# The Mourner's Book of Faith

# Faith

30 Days of Enlightenment

# The Mourner's Book of

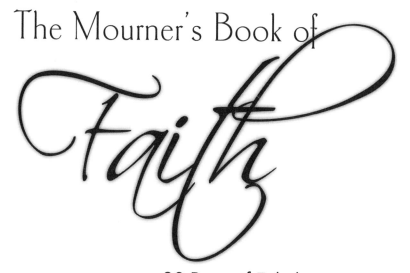

## 30 Days of Enlightenment

## ALAN D. WOLFELT, PH.D.

Companion
PRESS

*An imprint of the Center for Loss and Life Transition*

Fort Collins, Colorado

Companion Press is an imprint of the Center for Loss and Life Transition, 3735 Broken Bow Road, Fort Collins, Colorado 80526. www.centerforloss.com

Artwork by Christoph Kadur, www.istockphoto.com
Cover design and book layout by Angela P. Hollingsworth

Printed in Canada.


22 21 20 19 18 17 16 15 14 13          5 4 3 2 1


ISBN: 978-1-61722-162-0

# Introduction

*Listen to your life. See it for the fathomless mystery that it is. Touch, taste, smell your way to the holy and hidden heart of it because in the last analysis, all moments are sacred moments and life itself is grace.*

~ Frederick Buechner

When someone dies, faith often comes to the forefront. Big questions arise, like, "Where did she go? Does her soul live on, and if so, can she hear me or feel me? Will she meet God? Will we meet again?" It's natural to wonder about the afterlife. Death also has a way of quickly helping us put our priorities in order. You might be thinking about your own life on a grander scale, too, realizing what really matters to you and how you want to live out your life.

There's a chance you could also be questioning your faith and finding that your old beliefs no longer apply now that you have experienced the death of someone loved. You may even feel angry with God, or betrayed, and question how God could take him from you. Wrestling with faith is common when someone close to you dies.

You've heard the idea of blind faith. Actually, that's redundant because all faith is blind: Having faith means believing and trusting in something that "has no logical proof or material evidence." Yet believing in only what we can see and experience with our five physical senses is extremely limiting and deadens our hopes and inspirations.

Faith is a bridge that gets you from your now to your future. Right now your bridge might feel like a wobbly wooden pathway swinging over a great chasm, or it might seem as sturdy and transcendent as the Golden Gate, or somewhere in between. Regardless, to walk your bridge you must put one foot in front of the other, trusting with each step that it will support you. I hope this book will supply you with a few useful tools to help you shore up your own bridge of faith.

## About This Book

This book is the third in a series of daily meditation books I've written to give people a quick, regular touchstone to inspire, encourage, and enlighten them as they walk their grief journeys. The first book is *The Mourner's Book of Hope*, the second *The Mourner's Book of Courage*. I've found through my own experiences with death and loss, as well as through the experiences of hundreds of people I've companioned through grief, that hope, courage, and faith are essential to doing the hard work that grief and mourning demand.

My wish is that this book will serve as one of many companions you have on your walk with grief. As you read, imagine these words coming from a supportive friend, someone who wants to help you strengthen your faith—however you define it— during this difficult time. You will find 30 daily meditations along with inspirational quotes to help you explore your faith and define what it means to you as you grieve and mourn the loss of the person who died.

At the start, I gently encourage you to honor all the feelings that come with grief. It can be difficult to "sit in your wound" and let your emotions wash over you. It seems so much easier to stay busy and ignore them. After all, who wants to hurt? But you will find that as you honor your pain you will be able to move through it and learn to live and love fully once again.

Along the way I suggest that you allow yourself to question your faith and redefine what God means to you, both inside and outside the boundaries of religion. In my experience, those who do not search, do not find. So, if you need to question, allow yourself to question. And remember that mystery, which is the ancient name for God, is something to be pondered, not explained. It's my wish that you can create a working faith— one that gives you strength to not only get through the day, but to eventually feel flashes of joy, experience grace, see silver linings, and commune in a way that's meaningful for you with your divine spark.

## My Prayer For You

My prayer for you is that as you journey through grief you will tap into the power of your faith or spirituality. Having faith provides a solid base to launch from. You may not know exactly where you will land, but you have faith that you will be OK no matter what. Sometimes, that strength, that knowing, that *faith*, is the only thing that will keep you going on your darkest days.

I pray that you will be able to tap into the light of faith—to allow its warmth to sustain you. Faith and light are intrinsically tied throughout history in religious drawings, scripture, and even in more recent stories of people who have "died" and returned to life and report seeing a tunnel of light with someone loved or God waiting on the other side. Fill your life with as much light as you can. Feeling light does not deny your grief or dishonor the person who died. Let joy, love, peace, gratitude, and self-care enter your days and keep your feet on your bridge.

My prayer for you, finally, is that you find a way to pray that feels real and meaningful to you. Maybe that will be meditating, communing with nature, talking to the person who died each night, getting down on your knees, attending a traditional service, or a combination of all of these things and more. It doesn't matter what it is, just so that it centers you, soothes your soul, and helps you connect with your faith in yourself and your world.

Blessings to you on your journey. I hope we meet one day.

# Day 1

## Feel Your Loss

*A star falls from the sky and into your hands. Then it seeps through your veins and swims inside your blood and becomes every part of you. And then you have to put it back into the sky. And it's the most painful thing you'll ever have to do and that you've ever done. But what's yours is yours. Whether it's up in the sky or here in your hands.*

~ C. JoyBell C.

*Verily, with hardship, there is relief.*

~ Quran 94:6

Someone you love has died, and more than likely you feel torn apart. It's as if someone literally removed a part of you, and where that part used to be there is now just a hole. It's empty, dark, lonely, and uncomfortable—and most of all, it's painful.

I am sorry you are feeling this pain of loss, for I have felt it myself. I commend you for not avoiding your pain. It is tempting, when we hurt so much, to try to patch ourselves up quickly, yet this does not work. Pain and grief have a way of demanding our attention. It's best to grab the hand of faith and walk into your pain. It is by moving through your pain that you will—slowly, eventually—reconcile and integrate your loss.

Of course in the early days, weeks, and months of your loss, your pain might be overwhelming. You might constantly feel the deep sadness that comes from living life without the person who died. During these times, remember to take breaks from your grief. Dose your pain by doing things that soothe and comfort you. Sit in nature, take baths, lay yourself down for naps, and spend time with people you love.

In many of my books I outline the "Six Needs of Mourning." The second of the six needs is "Embrace the pain of the loss." It is a vital step in your journey of grief and mourning. Even though it is easier to stay busy and avoid, repress, or push away your pain, I encourage you to fully experience your pain

*Remember, an easy question can have an easy answer. But a hard question must have a hard answer. And for the hardest questions of all, there may be no answer—except faith.*

~ Charles Sheffield

as much and as often as you can. Maybe today you can only touch it fully for 15 minutes. That's OK.

Sharing your pain with others is cathartic, as is sharing your joys. Make a date with a good friend—one who will listen and not try to take your pain away—to share photo albums of your life with the person who died. Tell her stories of how you met, the special times you shared, and what you love and miss about this special person. Let the tears flow, and welcome words and gestures of comfort. Joining a grief support group is another way to embrace your pain.

Your pain will never completely go away, but if you actively mourn, over time it will soften. Buried pain, on the other hand, will not. Repressed grief can lead to depression. If you hold in your pain, you will feel stuck, and you will not live and love fully. Have faith that moving through your pain is the best thing to do.

*We never know when our last day on earth will be. So, love with full sincerity, believe with true faith, and hope with all of your might. Better to have lived in truth and discovered life than to have lived half-heartedly and died long before you ever ceased breathing.*
~ Cristina Marrero

## Personal Reflections on Faith

Each night before going to bed, say out loud, "I have faith in my pain and the wisdom and healing it brings." Sit in silence for a moment, and visualize your heart opening and your mind unfolding.

_____

_____

_____

_____

_____

_____

_____

_____

_____

_____

_____

_____

# Day 2

## Befriend Faith

*Faith is realizing that you always get what you need.*

~ Sri Sri Ravi Shankar

*Faith is the bird that feels the light and*
*sings when the dawn is still dark.*

~ Rabindranath Tagore

What does it mean to have faith? While the Merriam-Webster dictionary defines faith as a "belief and trust in, and loyalty to, God," it is much harder to define on a personal level. At its core, faith is trusting in something without concrete, tangible proof. Yet more so, I think of faith as a state of being—the honest, real place from which we operate and approach life. Faith brings together strong internal and external convictions and beliefs about how to live our daily lives, what happens after we die, and what we believe about God. Faith may be a hard concept for you to hold onto right now.

People who adhere to religious beliefs find comfort in the proclamations their religion makes about death and the afterlife. It is reassuring to imagine the person who died in heaven, sitting at the side of God. Many religions teach that the soul lives on. In the Hindu religion, the soul is reincarnated according to karma, or actions, in the previous life. Christian faith believes its followers have a forever place in heaven. What do you believe about faith and the afterlife?

In its simplest state, faith is like a wise companion walking beside you, sometimes taking your hand and stepping ahead to guide you. Befriend faith. Welcome the feelings of loving assurance that having faith brings. There is a famous Christian poem called "Footprints" that you've probably heard. In it, a person has a dream that she is walking the journey of her life with God, each making footprints in the sand. Yet at the lowest

*To have faith is to trust yourself to the water. When you swim you don't grab hold of the water, because if you do you will sink and drown. Instead you relax, and float.*

~ Alan Wilson Watts

points of this person's life, there is only one set of footprints. She asks, "Why when I needed you most, you have not been there for me?" God replies, "When you see only one set of footprints, it was then that I carried you."

Maybe your faith is not based in religion, but more in a belief in a higher power, a force of light and love in the world. When you tap into this power, you may feel faith that there is a higher order to things, and you generally have faith that things will turn out OK. Faith feeds your divine spark—your soul.

Whether you practice a religious faith or experience a more generally spiritual faith, I urge you to tap into it often during this time of loss. Let it counter your pain and carry you. Wrestle with it, if you need to. Either way, welcome faith as you would a friend.

*Faith is universal. Our specific methods for understanding it are arbitrary. Some of us pray to Jesus, some of us go to Mecca, some of us study subatomic particles. In the end we are all just searching for truth, that which is greater than ourselves.*

~ Dan Brown

## Personal Reflection on Faith

Take a minute to do a word association exercise around the word faith. What other words companion faith? The words trust, hope, and belief in God are all close cousins to faith. Create your own definition of what it means to have faith.

_____

_____

_____

_____

_____

_____

_____

_____

_____

_____

_____

# Day 3

## Contemplate God

*We need to find God, and he cannot be found in noise and restlessness. God is the friend of silence. See how nature—trees, flowers, grass—grows in silence; see the stars, the moon, and the sun, how they move in silence... We need silence to be able to touch souls.*

~ Mother Teresa

*All who call on God in true faith, earnestly from the heart, will certainly be heard, and will receive what they have asked and desired.*

~ Martin Luther

When you think about the word God, what comes to mind? Do you carry an image, as many of us did in our childhoods, of an old, wise man? Or is God more of a feeling or state of being for you? The dictionary defines God as "the supreme or ultimate reality: the Being perfect in power, wisdom, and goodness who is worshipped as creator and ruler of the universe." Do you adhere to the Christian God, the Islam Allah, the Bahá'í Baha, or the Jewish Yahweh? Or are your beliefs more spiritual, like the Unity movement's definition of God, which states: "God is Spirit, the loving source of all that is. God is the one power, all good, everywhere present, all wisdom. God is divine energy, continually creating, expressing, and sustaining all creation. In God, we live and move and have our being. God [is] Life, Light, Love, Substance, Principle, Law, and Universal Mind."

Is God in your view a loving God or a vengeful God? Do you fear punishment if you step out of line, or are you assured that you will be loved and forgiven for your missteps? A principle of faith in the Jewish religion is that God "will reward the good and punish the wicked" and that the "dead will be resurrected." Quakers believe that "God is love. The light of God is in every single person. A person who lets their life be guided by that light will achieve a full relationship with God. Everyone can have a direct, personal relationship with God." Adherers to Bahá'í believe in the "oneness of humanity" and the "common

*I believe in God, but not as one thing, not as an old man in the sky. I believe that what people call God is something in all of us.*

~ John Lennon

*God gave us the gift of life; it is up to us to give ourselves the gift of living well.*

~ Voltaire

origin and unity of purpose of all world religions." Finally, the Christian Bible states that "God is love."

It is important, during this time of grief, to consider what God means to you. If you don't believe in God, think about what having faith means to you. Ask yourself if you adhere to any universal truths. What are they? Do you believe people are basically good and kind? Do you believe that if you stay honest and live with integrity, you will find serenity and peace? Buddhists adhere to four noble truths established by Buddha on human suffering. One is Nirodha, which means "an end to suffering," where the mind experiences complete freedom and liberation, and Nirvana is reached.

Pin your faith on the beliefs that make sense to you at your core—ones that are positive and can carry you forward in your journey through grief and mourning. If you feel questions rising about faith and God, consider doing some exploring of the major religions and spiritual lenses of the world. Talk to your friends and family about their beliefs in God. Watch for common themes and truths that strike a chord. Start where you are and explore what God means to you.

## Personal Reflection on Faith

If you had to name five universal truths, what would they be? These ideas define your faith. Keep the ones that empower you to live and love fully for the rest of your days here on earth and consider redefining the rest.

_____

_____

_____

_____

_____

_____

_____

_____

_____

_____

_____

_____

_____

# Day 4

## Express Doubt

*Faith never stays put. It's always challenging, always questioning. That's what makes it real.*

~ Patrick Carman

*Doubt isn't the opposite of faith; it is an element of faith.*

~ Paul Tillich

Maybe you are wrestling with your faith after the death of your loved one. Death (and other significant losses too) shake our foundation and leave us unsure of where we stand in our beliefs. If you are wrestling with your faith right now, that's OK. If you are mad at God, be mad. If you are questioning God, question. Being angry at God, or having doubts about God, speaks of having a relationship with God in the first place. I've always said to myself, "God has been doing very well for some time now, so I think he can handle my anger."

You might find that others send you the message that showing your grief is a sign that your faith is weak. Maybe you have heard people say, "She's in a better place," or "It's God's will," or "God called her home," and these sayings feel like a dismissal of your grief and pain. These folks probably mean well and are trying to comfort you, but there is no denying that the message is that you shouldn't feel sad, and you shouldn't mourn. Yet faith and grief can, and should, coexist. You might find comfort in believing the person you love is in heaven yet at the same time miss her terribly. Feeling this pain is a sign of strength, not weakness. It's a necessary part of your journey through grief.

Maybe your faith feels like it's been turned upside-down. If you need a time-out from your long-held beliefs or your regular worship services, take it. Going into "exile" for a while can be a way to honor your healing. If people try to

*If faith never encounters doubt, if truth never struggles with error, if good never battles evil, how can faith know its own power? In my own pilgrimage, if I had to choose between a faith that has stared doubt in the eye and made it blink, or a naive faith that has never known the firing line of doubt, I will choose the former every time.*

~ Gary Parker

*Faith doesn't mean you never doubt. It only means you never act upon your doubts.*

~ Orson Scott Card

drag you to a place of worship and you don't want to go, dig your heels in and tell them you'll go when and if you're ready.

When you are ready, allow yourself to express your faith in varied ways. Attending a church, synagogue, mosque, or other place of worship, reading scripture, and praying are only a few ways to express your faith. Appreciating the beauty of nature, meditating, and expressing yourself through music are other ways to voice your faith. Remember, this is your unique passage through grief and loss. Control your own sail.

*Doubts are the ants in the pants of faith.*
*They keep it awake and moving.*

~ Frederick Buechner

*It's natural and perfectly OK to question your faith at this time. Having faith and openly mourning are not mutually exclusive. Being upset and openly mourning does not mean you are being "weak" in your faith. Remember the Bible quote that states, "Blessed are those who mourn, for they shall be comforted."*

~ Alan D. Wolfelt

## Personal Reflection on Faith

Are you experiencing doubt in God? Are some of the truths you've always carried feeling untrue to you now? Explore these feelings of doubt with a good listener or through writing, art, or another form of self-expression.

_____

_____

_____

_____

_____

_____

_____

_____

_____

_____

_____

# Day 5

## Adopt a Daily Spiritual Practice

*God is an unutterable sigh, planted
in the depths of the soul.*

~ Jean Paul Richter


*You have to grow from the inside out. None can
teach you, none can make you spiritual. There
is no other teacher but your own soul.*

~ Swami Vivekananda

Mourning is a spiritual journey of the heart and soul. When someone you love dies, you open to a world of feelings, emotions, and mystery. Your pain might feel as if it is cracking you open. Your open heart is a "well of reception" that invites your soul forward. Your soul is the primary essence of your true nature, your spirit self, your life force—what I call your "divine spark." Your divine spark has been muted by your suffering, but it never goes out. Feed it as best you can, every day.

One way to do this is to adopt a daily spiritual practice. For you, this could be praying each morning upon awakening or sitting in silence in nature each evening. Maybe it is more formal and involves going to a place of worship regularly and attending services and study groups. Or possibly it is informal, as in checking in with a best friend each night on how you are doing emotionally and spiritually.

We all fall into daily routines. Make it a part of your routine to commune with your spirit every day. If you are unsure where to start, ask others about their spiritual practices. Spend time with people who embody the faith you wish to live.

Remember, there is no right or wrong way to have a spiritual practice. Stop and ask yourself, "What feeds my divine spark? What makes me feel centered and balanced? What opens my spirit?" Get creative. Sit in a room surrounded by candles. Lie in the grass and gaze at the stars. Take a road trip to a remote,

*A man sooner or later discovers that he is the master-gardener of his soul, the director of his life.*

~ James Allen


*Live one moment at a time and that moment for God. Don't think of a holy life, for that will drown you by its immensity, but remember that a holy life is a series of holy moments.*

~ Anonymous

beautiful place. Visit a stupa or monastery and commune with the monks.

Sometimes spiritual practice happens on its own. In other words, our souls seek out what they need. Maybe driving home from work you have the urge to pull over and walk around a city lake or take off your shoes and wade into the ocean. Or maybe you want to build a fire in the middle of July or crank the music louder than you did as a teenager and lose yourself in its power. Do it. This is your soul, your divine spirit, asking for expression. Welcome its release.

Your spiritual understanding is yours and yours alone, even if you adhere to a certain faith. How you commune with your spirit or feed your divine spark is uniquely yours to decide.

## Personal Reflection on Faith

Just as you exercise and feed your body every day, exercise and feed your spirit. What is your soul yearning for today?

_____

_____

_____

_____

_____

_____

_____

_____

_____

_____

_____

_____

# Day 6

## Attend to Your Needs

*Be gentle with yourself. You are a child of the universe no less than the trees and the stars.*

~ Max Ehrmann

*The wound is the place where the Light enters you.*

~ Rumi

Sometimes when we are grieving we need to keep things simple. We need to slow down and honor ourselves and be where we are rather than trying to be where we think we should. Have you been feeling overwhelmed lately? Living through the loss of someone you love is one of the hardest experiences you will ever have. It's important that you go easy on yourself.

Rest. Take naps. Feed yourself healthy food. Allow for time to just be. If you need to cry, don't hold back. Your tears are sacred, and crying is naturally cleansing and healing. You may even find a need to keen—to wail loudly in lament for the dead. Or you may experience griefbursts at unexpected times or places. Don't be embarrassed or rattled by your emotions. Attend to your needs.

Make yourself the priority during this difficult time. Say no to invitations that do not appeal to you. Yet if you find that you desire to commune with others, make a call to a friend or seek out a support group or counselor. Isolating when you want to be with others locks your grief inside.

Release expectations others might have of you. For example, maybe you have always been the emotionally strong one in the family—the one everyone else relies on. Yet now it is you who needs comfort and support. Allow yourself to drop your old role and trust that others will step in to help you and that they will accept you and your feelings. To whom can you reach out

*The quality of mercy is not strained; It droppeth as the gentle rain from heaven upon the place beneath. It is twice blessed—It blesseth him that gives, and him that takes.*

~ William Shakespeare

*For me, singing sad songs often has a way of healing a situation. It gets the hurt out in the open, into the light, out of the darkness.*

~ Reba McEntire

who will accept your grief without trying to fix it? Make this person a companion through your grief journey.

Maybe your loved one's death is new, and you are tempted to stay busy and ignore your grief. That is fine for a little while. Sometimes pain is too big to take in all at once. Yet, when you are ready, stop and feel your grief and express it through mourning—even if you can only do so for snippets of time.

During this time, your body, mind, and soul need healing. There are eight universal healing principles that cross almost all cultural lines. In brief, they are eating a balanced diet, getting regular exercise, taking time for fun and play, experiencing music and chanting, receiving love and touch, engaging in interests and hobbies, experiencing nature and beauty, and expressing faith. Which of these principles appeals to you right now? Consider how you can experience one of these today.

## Personal Reflection on Faith

Ask yourself: "What do I need right now?" If you need comfort, ask for it from a trusted friend. If you need rest, allow yourself to crawl into bed regardless of the time of day. If you need nourishment, visit the supermarket and splurge on a rare treat. Trust your intuition. It is the voice of your soul and will guide you to fulfill your need.

_____

_____

_____

_____

_____

_____

_____

_____

_____

_____

_____

_____

# Day 7

## Release Pain

*And remember this most of all: when it is darkest,
that is when you can see the stars most clearly.*

~ Kathleen McGowan


*When God is going to do something wonderful,
He or She always starts with a hardship;
when God is going to do something amazing,
He or She starts with an impossibility.*

~ Anne Lamott

When someone you love dies, you feel the loss down to the core of your being. It rattles you, sometimes senseless. Even though it is hard, it's important to not only feel your pain, but release it. Grief comes naturally; mourning demands a more conscious effort. How do you release the pain of your loss? How do you mourn?

Start by sitting in your wound. When we hurt, our first instinct is to turn away from what's causing the pain—to stay busy, repress, or avoid thoughts and feelings of the person who has died. Know that some people will try to help you do this. They'll offer such advice as "keep your chin up," or "stay strong." Please know that true strength lies in facing your pain—walking right into it rather than around it. Yes, it will hurt. It will be hard. But when you feel your pain and release it through mourning, you will avoid getting emotionally stuck in a land of undefined sadness, irritability, or dissatisfaction with life.

One way to actively mourn is to keep a journal and record your grief feelings honestly and fully. Another way is to haul out photo albums and videos of your loved one or visit places you enjoyed together. You could also take on passions of the person who died and try activities he or she loved.

It's also important to physically release your grief. Cry, wail, scream, sigh loudly, and talk to others who will listen. Or

*The greatest act of faith some days is to simply get up and face another day.*

~ Amy Gatliff

*Faith doesn't get you around problems [and difficulties] in life and relationships, it gets you through them.*

~ Jonathan Anthony Burkett

release your pain through exercise—lifting weights, running, biking, dancing, or kickboxing may bring relief.

Consider displaying items that remind you of the person who died. Maybe it's a prized possession like artwork, books, a religious symbol, a special piece of the person's clothing, or something precious that she made. If you'd like to, carry with you something of hers such as a piece of jewelry. These are called "linking objects." As you grieve and mourn over time, your need for linking objects will probably lessen. But keep them as long as you want.

In some religious faiths the funeral is seen as the place to release your pain. Yes, this is a good place to start—especially if it honors your loved one in a meaningful way. But it's just the beginning of your grief journey. I suggest you not use the word "closure" as it relates to the goals of a funeral. Actually, funerals help you get off to a meaningful start with your mourning.

Honor your pain. At first, it might feel like shock or disbelief. Later, you might feel as if you are "going crazy." Feelings of anxiety, panic, and fear may also be a part of your grief experience—even anger, hate, blame, guilt, or regret. All these feelings are a normal part of grieving and mourning. Open to them as best you can, and have faith that you will not always feel this way.

## Personal Reflection on Faith

What instinctively feels like the right way to release your pain?
Do you need to talk about it, act it out, or sit alone and wail?
Maybe you are filled with spiritual questions and need the
guidance of a religious or spiritual leader? Take action, today.

_____

_____

_____

_____

_____

_____

_____

_____

_____

_____

_____

# Day 8

## Make Use of Ritual

*Ritual is necessary for us to know anything.*

~ Ken Kesey

*Faith is not so much something we
believe; faith is something we live.*

~ Joseph B. Wirthlin

So much of faith is unspoken. Intuition is often the voice of our spirit. We may intuitively know that listening to music feels healing or that walking in nature centers us. We may do these things without realizing that it's at the urging of our divine spark. Rituals like these, and those more defined, allow our souls to speak wordlessly. If you feel an innate sense that your feelings around the death of your loved one continue to be unreconciled, and that words feel inadequate, consider having a ritual.

Rituals, alone or with others, can heal without your conscious mind precisely knowing why. If you have an urge to perform a ritual, trust it despite what your head might say about it being silly or you feeling foolish.

People create rituals in many ways, both formal and informal. Maybe you have fallen into a ritual of talking out loud to the person who died when you first wake up in the morning, or going to a favorite place the two of you enjoyed together. Honor these spontaneous, unconscious rituals.

You may also feel a need for a more formal ritual. Yes, the funeral helped serve this purpose, but you can have many other rituals and ceremonies, as many as you need and desire. Maybe you feel an urge to recreate a funeral of sorts—a way to commune with the person who died or honor his spirit with others. Elements of ritual through the ages have

*Faith is an oasis in the heart which will never be reached by the caravan of thinking.*

~ Kahlil Gibran

*Faith is a power of its own, and one even more elusive and difficult to define than magic.*

~ Jim Butcher

included music—drums, bells, chimes, etc.—candles, nature, cloth or other items of beauty that were significant in his life, photographs, writings, and storytelling. As with rituals, these ceremonies help you recall the person who died and express your pain, even silently. Often after a ceremony or planned ritual, people feel a sense of relief, peace, or even joy.

Rituals can be very simple, such as wearing a symbol of mourning. In centuries past, mourners often made wreaths or jewelry out of locks of hair that belonged to the person who died. Some cultures wore black armbands to express their grief. Maybe you want to carry or wear an item that belonged to the person who died. Or if he loved gardening, you could make a ritual out of planting a favorite tree or flower variety or placing a wind chime or garden sculpture to represent his spirit.

Rituals help you heal. Ongoing ritual or ceremony can help you remember and integrate the loss into your heart and soul. Jewish services allow for a practice called Yizkor, where anyone who has experienced a loss can stay and give a "remembering prayer." Its purpose is to create a sacred time and place for mourning. Express your grief and mourning through rituals, big and small. Place your faith in their transcendent, healing power.

## Personal Reflection on Faith

If you were to create a ceremony or ritual to release your grief or to honor your loved one's spirit, what might you do?

---

---

---

---

---

---

---

---

---

---

---

---

---

# Day 9

## Talk to God (or Your Higher Power)

*When every hope is gone, "when helpers fail and comforts flee," I find that help arrives somehow from I know not where. Supplication, worship, prayer are no superstition; they are acts more real than the acts of eating, drinking, sitting, or walking. It is no exaggeration to say that they alone are real, all else is unreal.*

~ Mahatma Gandhi

There are many ways to talk to God, commune with the Divine, or tap into the all-powerful presence or energy that guides all life. You can get down on your knees and pray to God, or you can sit in nature or under the stars and absorb the enormity of the earth, heavens, and all that is. If you believe your divine spark or soul is part of a larger whole, then experience the power of communing with that whole by conversing with it through words, actions, and even silence.

Praying, singing, shouting, lamenting, keening, and crying out to God are all ways to actively mourn. There are medical studies that support the power of prayer. Prayer has been shown to help people heal and reach emotional equilibrium. Muslims are required to pray five times a day to reach spiritual enlightenment.

Tell God about how it feels to live without the person who died. Ask questions—especially the ones that start with "why" when it comes to life and death. Curse God if you need to—God can take it. Ask for strength to embrace your pain. Ask how you can slowly go forward, always remembering your past as you discover renewed meaning in your life. Explore your hopes for the future and those the person who died held for you.

Besides offering up words, you can also talk to God through journaling; attending worship services; reading meaningful texts; being wowed by the beauty of nature; repeating a

*When I called, you answered me; you made me bold and stouthearted.*

~ Psalm 138:3

*Why must people kneel down to pray? If I really wanted to pray, I'll tell you what I'd do. I'd go out into a great big field all alone or in the deep, deep woods and I'd look up into the sky—up, up, up—into that lovely blue sky that looks as if there was no end to its blueness. And then I'd just feel a prayer.*

~ L.M. Montgomery

mantra, prayer or quote; meditating; and singing poignant lyrics to songs.

Get in the habit of talking with God every day. Talk about your feelings of grief—especially those you most want to hold in. Maybe you feel some guilt, regret, or self-blame about your loved one's death. These are common feelings. You may have a case of the "if-onlys" and wish that you handled some things differently. Or maybe you feel guilty for feeling relief that your loved one died after a long illness. Express yourself without feelings of shame. Know that God does not judge you and only wants to hear your words and help you heal. Trust that your feelings are not right or wrong. Have faith that the release of your words will help you find renewed hope and healing. Have faith that mourning will eventually help you reconcile your loss. Reconciliation is when you will feel a sense of coming out on the other side and hope for a new start.

*Prayer need not be in words, but rather in thought and attitude...*

~ Abdu'l-Bahá

## Personal Reflection on Faith

How do you "pray"? There is no right or wrong way. Find a method that feels right for you. What do you want to say to God today?

_____

_____

_____

_____

_____

_____

_____

_____

_____

_____

_____

_____

_____

# Day 10

## Lead with Your Heart (Not Your Head)

*But what of faith? What of fidelity and loyalty? Complete trust? Faith is not granted by tangible proof. It comes from the heart and the soul.*

~ R.A. Salvatore

*Faith and science, I have learned, are two sides of the same coin, separated by an expanse so small, but wide enough that one side can't see the other. They don't know they are connected.*

~ Mary E. Pearson

We live in a world that relies on logic more than faith, intuition, emotion, and mystery. Science and logic are important to advance our society and better our lives, but they do little good when someone we love has died. In the realm of death, loss, and grief, it's best to let our hearts, rather than our heads, lead. After all, emotions are the language of the soul.

Throughout life we constantly praise people's "head smarts" rather than their "heart smarts." Yet in the end, when we honor those who have died, little is said about how smart they were, or how successful they were as businesspeople or how much money they made. Rather, people talk about their character, whether they gave to others or the community, and how much they loved and were loved in return.

What is your heart saying these days? If someone you love has recently died, most likely it is breaking. Don't deny your heart's desire to express your deep sadness. Maybe your heart is pounding fast and is scared. If your future was tied to the person who died, you may fear what's to come, or you may be wondering how you can possibly go on without her. You may feel like your foundation is no longer solid. These feelings are natural. Have faith that a new day will come, and once again you will find your balance. You will not always hurt as much as you do now.

*Reason is in fact the path to faith, and faith takes over when reason can say no more.*

~ Thomas Merton

*I am not moved by what I see. I am not moved by what I feel. I am moved only by what I believe.*

~ Smith Wigglesworth

What soothes your heart? Often, the heart doesn't speak in words but rather in beauty and light. For example, watching a yellow cottonwood tree drop its leaves and seeing them flutter to the ground may restore and calm your heart. Feeling the heat of the sun as it penetrates your body might recharge your heart, or hearing a moving piece of music might awaken it.

What makes your heart feel hopeful? Is it knowing that someday you will be reunited with your loved one? Is it a belief that her soul lives on? Do you gain strength from the idea that she is "up there" smiling down on you and wishing you joy, love, and healing? Maybe you feel hope when you do things you know your loved one enjoyed or fulfill some activities that brought her meaning. Maybe you feel hope in forging a deep connection and understanding with others. Let your heart speak in these intangible ways.

The voice of your heart can't be heard above the din of constant going, constant distraction, and constant busy-ness. Invite your heart to speak by creating times of silence in your days. Welcome "heart-speak" by spending time in nature. You may not hear words, but you will feel messages in the form of truth, hope, and calm.

## Personal Reflection on Faith

Today, and every day forward, turn off the television and spend some time sitting in silence. Consider it "heart-speak" time.

# Day 11

## Fall Back and Let Others Catch You

*I think if I've learned anything about friendship, it's to hang in, stay connected, fight for them, and let them fight for you. Don't walk away, don't be distracted, don't be too busy or tired, don't take them for granted. Friends are part of the glue that holds life and faith together.*

~ Jon Katz

*You can never really know someone completely. That's why it's the most terrifying thing in the world, really—taking someone on faith, hoping they'll take you on faith too. It's such a precarious balance. It's a wonder we do it at all. And yet....*

~ Libba Bray

When you experience a death or another earthshaking hardship, things get real fast. Making pleasantries can be taxing because their lightness is in such contrast with the realness and rawness of your grief. What you need right now is deep connection with others. Honesty is your ticket. Let others know that you are hurting and need their support. If you feel like you have been stripped bare by your loss, that you are raw and vulnerable, don't be afraid to show this to the people who care about you. Trust that they will be there for you. Have faith that they will catch you.

In my earlier books I have outlined Six Needs of Mourning. Number six is: "Let others help you—now and always." You cannot, and should not, grieve alone. In fact, your capacity to heal is intrinsically tied to how much you let others support you. The more you share your grief, the more you will heal. Have faith in other people. Have faith in humanity and the goodness of others. There are people out there who want to bear witness to your pain and treat you with care.

Right now you need people to lean on—friends, relatives, a counselor, a support group, or a combination of all of these. Needing others, contrary to the mourning-avoiding messages of our society to "get over" your grief and "move on," is a healthy human need. Use your intuition and seek out those individuals you think will be comfortable sitting with you

*You must not lose faith in humanity. Humanity is like an ocean; if a few drops of the ocean are dirty, the ocean does not become dirty.*

~ Mahatma Gandhi

*Some people are angels sent to you by God at your weakest moments.*

~ Megan Wilson

in your wound. People who see your grief as something to overcome or fix are not the right ones to rely upon.

Of course there will be times when you want a friend to distract you from your pain, but a true friend in grief is one who will enter your pain with you, letting you lead the way and determine the course. I like to think of these people as companions—people who will walk with you through your grief journey, who will hear your pain, your anger, and your laments without judgment or discomfort. If you do not have someone like this, seek help from a professional counselor or attend a grief support group through your local hospice center or hospital.

Have you ever played the trust game, in which you are blindfolded and instructed to fall back and let the person standing behind you catch you? It takes guts and a lot of faith to do this. Yet consider that you are already primed to fall back and be caught. In some ways your grief and pain have opened you to this. After all, what are your options? If you don't fall back into your grief and into the arms of others, you risk staying stuck in your pain or stuffing it where it will remain unreconciled. Either way you will be left feeling discontent.

Fall back. Accept help from others. Be raw. Be vulnerable. And have trust and faith that there is strength in doing so.

## Personal Reflection on Faith

Whom can you call, right now, who will stop and take the time to listen to you? Tell him you need support. Consider setting up a weekly coffee date with her.

_____

_____

_____

_____

_____

_____

_____

_____

_____

_____

_____

_____

_____

# Day 12

## Recharge with Meaning

*Faith is not about finding meaning in the world,
there may be no such thing—faith is the belief
in our capacity to create meaningful lives.*

~ Terry Tempest Williams


*The reason birds can fly and we can't is simply because
they have perfect faith, for to have faith is to have wings.*

~ J.M. Barrie

When we do things that matter to us, we feel assured that we are on the right path, and our faith in our lives is restored. You may feel as if the only person who really mattered to you is gone. Yet there are other people and activities in your life that probably bring you joy and meaning. What are they? Sometimes going through the motions and doing something that used to bring you joy is enough to help you realign and rebalance your life. Have faith that doing something meaningful can restore you, at least temporarily.

What brings meaning to your life? Is it attending a religious service? Spending time with a loved one? Is it taking on a new project, hobby, sport, or relationship and finding success and satisfaction? Meaning can be found in taking risks—in figuring out what is missing in your life and taking action to fill the gap. If you intuitively feel there is something you want to do or a change you want to make—and it feels like a positive force, muster your courage and give it a go.

I also encourage you to reassess your faith. You might naturally be doing this anyway. When the person you love died, a part of you died with him. You might feel buoyed by your religious faith and sure about the meaning of life, or you might find your religious faith no longer offers comfort or security. If so, maybe it's time to explore your religious faith further by attending a spiritual retreat or trying out a new place of worship, spiritual movement, or way of thinking.

*Out of the cacophony of random suffering and chaos that can mark human life, a "life artist" sees or creates a symphony of meaning and order. A life of wholeness does not depend on what we experience. Wholeness depends on how we experience our lives.*

~ Desmond Tutu

*Faith is walking face-first and full-speed into the dark. If we truly knew all the answers in advance as to the meaning of life and the nature of God and the destiny of our souls, our belief would not be a leap of faith and it would not be a courageous act of humanity; it would just be...a prudent insurance policy.*

~ Elizabeth Gilbert

When someone you love dies, you naturally question the meaning and purpose of life. You might be asking God, "How could you let this happen?" or "Why did you take her/him?" Loss on such a large scale can leave you feeling powerless. In my Six Needs of Mourning, "Search for Meaning" is number five. It's perfectly natural to be questioning your faith at this time. You might do this for weeks, even months. Over time, have faith that you will once again find meaning in your continued living.

To encourage a return to a sense of purpose, take the opportunity to have meaningful experiences. Accept and give love. Start where it's easy—with children. Let their light and pure spirits fill you with hope. Allow yourself to laugh. Studies show that laughter helps you heal by releasing chemicals in the brain that turn off your stress hormones. Even in the midst of constant pain, you might find something that strikes you funny. Don't hold back. Joy and laughter do not take away from the seriousness of your grief or your loss. Rather, they provide a needed respite and release—and most of all, they restore hope and faith that life is still worth living.

## Personal Reflection on Faith

Even if you are hurting and your pain is raw, take a few minutes each day to do something that brings you meaning and restores your faith. Spend time with someone who matters to you, be in nature, or create something—a painting, a poem, a batch of cookies for a neighbor, a home repair, or anything that gives you a sense of accomplishment and forward movement.

# Day 13

## Tap into Your Strength

*The eternal God is your refuge, and underneath are the everlasting arms.*

~ Deuteronomy 33:27

*Faith gives you an inner strength and a sense of balance and perspective in life.*

~ Gregory Peck

When people go through hard times, we sometimes hear them say, "I found a strength I never knew I had." When you experience a significant loss or endure great pain, there's a sense of being stripped down to the basics of who you are. You learn to cope, even when you don't think you can go on. Even if you can't imagine how, you get through one day after the next. Slowly, surely, you gain real strength.

What in the past has helped you endure hard times? Was it your faith that God, or a higher power, is watching over you? Was it your ability to seek out support and find comfort in others, knowing inherently that doing so is a sign of strength, not weakness? Was it a belief that you will be OK no matter what, a belief in divine order, or a faith that "this too, shall pass"? Maybe it was your willingness to trust your intuition and let it guide you to what you need to heal—a knowing when to say no and when to say yes, or sensing when to follow a spontaneous urge for self-care, like sitting in nature. Tap into these core beliefs of your faith now. Let them buoy you.

Also, be reassured that the spirit of the person who died, whether you believe her soul lives on or not, would want you to heal and find joy once again. At the core, that person's love for you was pure. She would want to see you release your pain, be washed by it, release it, and thrive. If you so believe, imagine your loved one smiling down on you. Imagine the

*It isn't for the moment you are struck that you need courage, but for that long uphill climb back to sanity and faith and security.*

~ Anne Morrow Lindbergh

*Be faithful in small things because it is in them that your strength lies.*

~ Mother Teresa

warmth of the sun or the rustle of the leaves as messages of love, gentleness, and strength from her to you.

You are stronger than you may think. Know that strength does not mean a quick recovery from grief and mourning. Acting "strong," as if you are not hurt and you don't need care, will only cause you to deny your grief feelings. If others congratulate you for keeping your grief "under control," know that this is a common misperception in our grief-avoidant society. Death is not always a comfortable topic for people. Some people are simply not strong enough to handle your grief. Find a companion with whom you can let it all out— someone who can sit with you and listen rather than cut you off and brush your grief away. If you do not experience your grief and actively mourn, you risk living an unfulfilled life where you expend too much energy trying to avoid your pain rather than reconciling it and feeling an inner peace.

Better to live, and feel, fully—even if it is messy, even if it hurts. Tap into your inner strength. Wear it as a talisman as you walk through the wilderness of your grief.

## Personal Reflection on Faith

What gives your soul steadfastness? What rights your world?
Incorporate these beliefs and actions into your everyday in the
form of an affirmation or prayer for strength.

_____

_____

_____

_____

_____

_____

_____

_____

_____

_____

_____

_____

# Day 14

## Let Your Healing Unfold

*I cannot think of a single advantage I've ever gained from being in a hurry. But a thousand broken and missed things, tens of thousands, lie in the wake of all the rushing.... Through all that haste I thought I was making up time. It turns out I was throwing it away.*

~ Ann Voskamp

*Maybe that's why life is so precious. No rewind or fast forward...just patience and faith.*

~ Cristina Marrero

When something hurts or is uncomfortable, you may have an urge to rush through it and get it over with. Unfortunately, this doesn't work with grief and mourning. Grief has no timetable and doesn't progress in a predictable, orderly way. Honor yourself, and your healing, by taking your grief at face value—by opening to what it brings and trusting the process.

Elisabeth Kübler-Ross did some extraordinary work on death and dying. She listed five stages of grief: denial, anger, bargaining, depression, and acceptance. Unfortunately, people have incorrectly assumed that her stages occur in a linear fashion. There's an idea that once you finish one, you are done with it and move on to the next. This isn't true with grief. Grief is more of a spiral, in which you may experience a certain feeling, say sadness, at one point then circle back to it again. You are also likely to experience several emotions at the same time.

Be patient with your unique grief journey. No two people experience the exact same path when it comes to grief and healing. Trust your own process, and let it take as long as it takes. What you are feeling is not something to be solved but something to be experienced—to walk right into and cross to the other side. It may take weeks, months, even years for you to integrate the loss of your loved one. Throw away the clock and let your healing unfold naturally.

*One often has to do what they have to do in order to do what they want to do; however if you only do what you want to do, then you will never do what you have to do!*

~ C. Moorer

*Faith is like love: it does not let itself be forced.*

~ Arthur Schopenhauer

Besides letting your healing unfold, let your new life—a life without the person you love—unfold as well. You are probably enduring a number of secondary losses besides your primary loss of the person who died. These losses can be broken down into three areas: 1) loss of self, 2) loss of security, and 3) loss of meaning. With loss of self, you might feel as if a part of you died too. You may have to rethink your identity. You may have gone from being a wife to a widow, for example—and all the losses that implies. Security might be lost emotionally (as a source of support is gone), physically (if you now live alone), or financially. Also, your daily routines, if you lived with the person, have to be adjusted. Finally, you might lose meaning by feeling unsure of your future, questioning your faith, finding it hard to feel joy, and wondering why or how you will go on.

Acknowledge these losses and the redefining that they bring. While it may seem hard to believe, you will find your feet again. You will reestablish yourself and define a new future. Let the healing around each of these losses unfold in its own time.

Explore a working faith—one that provides comfort and clarity and makes sense to you today.

## Personal Reflection on Faith

Which facets of grief have you been feeling the most lately?
Express them as best you can.

_____

_____

_____

_____

_____

_____

_____

_____

_____

_____

_____

_____

_____

# Day 15

## Open to the Unknown

*Faith is a place of mystery, where we find the courage to believe in what we cannot see and the strength to let go of our fear of uncertainty.*

~ Brené Brown

*Why did they believe? Because they saw miracles. Things one man took as chance, a man of faith took as a sign. A loved one recovering from disease, a fortunate business deal, a chance meeting with a long-lost friend. It wasn't the grand doctrines or the sweeping ideals that seemed to make believers out of men. It was the simple magic in the world around them.*

~ Brandon Sanderson

What happens after we die is a mystery. Is there a heaven or hell? Are we judged? Is our life played out before our eyes—including all the joys and pains we have felt and caused others to feel? Is there a bright tunnel, with our loved ones waiting on the other side? Is there instant forgiveness for our sins? What is God like, and what role does God play in our lives? Are there angels? Will we meet Jesus, or Buddha, or Mohammed? Is there a divine plan for all of us, or do we orchestrate our own lives? Or is there nothingness? It's all a big unknown. Religious scholars and mystics have sought answers to these questions since time immemorial.

You might have strong beliefs or a religious faith that provides you with answers, or you might be re-asking these questions since the death. Both Buddhists and Hindus believe that souls are reincarnated—the Buddhist as a new soul in a new body, the Hindu as the same soul in a new body. Muslims believe our paths are predetermined by God.

It's natural to ask questions. It's understandable that you want to understand what has happened and know the person who died is "OK." Yet at some point, instead of seeking understanding, I urge you to "stand under" the mystery of life.

When you open to the unknown, you allow opportunities for mystery to come into your life. Let your faith, and hope, lead you. Keep your eyes, ears, and heart open. If you believe your

*Have you ever noticed that when your mind is awakened or drawn to someone new, that person's name suddenly pops up everywhere you go? My friend Sophie calls it coincidence, and Mr. Simpless, my parson friend, calls it grace. He thinks that if one cares deeply about someone or something new, one throws a kind of energy out into the world, and "fruitfulness" is drawn in.*

~ Mary Ann Shaffer

*It is not easy to convey a sense of wonder to another. It's the very nature of wonder to catch us off guard, to circumvent expectations and assumptions. Wonder can't be packaged, and it can't be worked up. It requires some sense of being there and some sense of engagement.*

~ Eugene H. Peterson

loved one's spirit lives on, invite his spirit to sit beside you or send you a sign that he feels joy in the afterlife. Remind yourself of your him by displaying photos or placing items that hold meaning around your house or your garden. Displaying objects that represent the person invites his spirit to accompany you.

I have companioned hundreds of people who tell stories of feeling their loved one's presence standing next to them or walking beside them, of smelling a scent connected to the person who died out-of-the-blue, or hearing encouraging statements or a song in their head without any provocation. If you have experienced this type of thing, accept it as a gift of comfort from your loved one. Even if your religious beliefs teach that such experiences are impossible, know that you are not being irrational or going crazy. See these experiences that provide an intimate connection to those who have gone before you as sacred and as an organic expression of the soul. Welcome them open-heartedly.

Contemplating the unknown and exploring your beliefs about the afterlife can bring comfort. You may never have all the answers, but you might find some nuggets of truth that feel real for you.

# Personal Reflection on Faith

What did your religious upbringing teach you about the afterlife? What do you believe today?

_____

_____

_____

_____

_____

_____

_____

_____

_____

_____

_____

_____

_____

# Day 16

## Feel Grateful

*Gratitude unlocks the fullness of life. It turns what we have into enough, and more. It turns denial into acceptance, chaos into order, confusion into clarity. It can turn a meal into a feast, a house into a home, a stranger into a friend.*

~ Melody Beattie

*To be grateful is to recognize the Love of God in everything He has given us—and He has given us everything. Every breath we draw is a gift of His love, every moment of existence is a grace, for it brings with it immense graces from Him. Gratitude therefore takes nothing for granted, is never unresponsive, is constantly awakening to new wonder and to praise of the goodness of God. For the grateful person knows that God is good, not by hearsay but by experience. And that is what makes all the difference.*

~ Thomas Merton

Gratitude is a powerful healing tool. Feeling grateful for our lives—even just the small things that bring us pleasure—calms us and reassures us that all is well. Gratitude gives us strength to go on when we don't feel like we can.

If you have recently experienced the death of someone loved, you may be thinking, "What could I possibly feel grateful for?" That is understandable. Start small. Consider the everyday, ordinary things that give you joy. Maybe it's watching the squirrels chase each other in the yard, seeing the sun set as you drive home from work, or getting a call from your child, grandchild, niece, or nephew. When you see something that offers peace, beauty, or calm, say a quick, "Thank you, Creator." As with love and forgiveness, gratitude holds great power to heal and set the world right.

By reminding yourself what is right in your life, you give your body, mind, and spirit a chance to reset on a positive course. It is like pushing the restart button—an opportunity to stop a negative spiral and begin again.

At our base, we are energy. If you have been grieving for a while and feel stuck in your grief and the insurmountable loss of someone you love, strive to change your thinking to more positive thoughts about your situation. If all your energy is going to feeling your lack, your sense of lack will grow. I am in no way suggesting you deny your feelings of grief, sadness, and

*Can you see the holiness in those things you take for granted—a paved road or a washing machine? If you concentrate on finding what is good in every situation, you will discover that your life will suddenly be filled with gratitude, a feeling that nurtures the soul.*

~ Rabbi Harold Kushner

*Saying thank you is more than good manners. It is good spirituality.*

~ Alfred Painter

loss. Rather, I am suggesting you give yourself a break from them, now and then, and allow a chance for a more positive flow of energy to come forward. Seek out richness and beauty each day, and be awed by their power.

You might consider keeping a gratitude journal—an ongoing list of things you feel grateful for each day. Or, commit to saying a brief gratitude prayer or affirmation upon awaking or retiring. A simple prayer that starts with, "Today I look forward to…" or "Today I am grateful for…" can either set the course for the day or help you sleep more peacefully at night. Saying a gratitude prayer is a way to create an immediate connection to God.

Feeling grateful can provide the faith that everything will be OK, that life is worth living. Gratitude's side effects are hope and a sense of renewal. Feeling thankful opens the door for love, passion, and self-fulfillment. And, of course, faith. What are you grateful for today?

## Personal Reflection on Faith

Write a short gratitude prayer that you can say out loud every day. If it is hard to write one, search for one on the Internet that rings true for you, and incorporate it into your life.

# Day 17

## Bathe in Grace

*It is unearned love—the love that goes before, that greets us on the way. It's the help you receive when you have no bright ideas left, when you are empty and desperate and have discovered that your best thinking and most charming charm have failed you. Grace is the light or electricity or juice or breeze that takes you from that isolated place and puts you with others who are as startled and embarrassed and eventually grateful as you are to be there.*

~ Anne Lamott

*When grace moves in...guilt moves out.*

~ Max Lucado

Grace is a hard concept to understand. The dictionary defines grace as "merited divine assistance given humans for their regeneration or sanctification." What does that really mean? Let's break it down some more. Sanctity means "holiness, sacredness," so sanctification means a state of holiness or sacredness. This definition of grace then could be interpreted as moments when God or the Divine steps in and offer guidance or signs to help us feel holy and sacred. Grace, then, in real terms, could be a sense of awe, a moment of inspiration that all is forgiven, that we are all loved children of God, and that all is well. Grace might be a moment in which God places a hand on our shoulders to guide us, to reassure us, or even to celebrate us.

In the Bible, Jesus shows grace through acts of healing—a literal laying on of hands to heal the crippled or ill. In Buddhism, while there isn't a direct translation for grace, it could exist in the transformation that karma brings.

During a challenging period of my life, I was driving down a country road on a beautiful fall day. I was feeling great sadness over a recent loss, and I looked up at a row of large cottonwood trees. Something about the way the trees swayed and how the light reflected off their yellow leaves felt so profound that I was left with a strong sense of peace—more like a recognition that I had just received a gift of peace from God. The message was one of forgiveness and love—and a lesson that all of life is a flow, a rhythm, and all I needed to do was lean back into that rhythm of the trees, the river, my blood, and my breath. I was

*It is the tenderness that breaks our hearts. The loveliness that leaves us stranded on the shore, watching the boats sail away. It is the sweetness that makes us want to reach out and touch the soft skin of another person. And it is the grace that comes to us, undeserving though we may be.*

~ Robert Goolrick

*Grace doesn't depend on suffering to exist, but where there is suffering, you will find grace in many facets and colors.*

~ W. Paul Young

stuck, but a bolt of grace gave me a chance to see my life in a new light.

I have since read that grace is an experience that you immediately recognize as a pure connection to the vibration of the Universe or God. I could not agree more.

Open to moments of grace—those flashes of feeling that you are one with God or being touched by God—as you face the pain and grief of your loss. Create opportunities for grace to find you, whether it is walking through an art museum and "feeling" the beauty in the paintings, being in nature, attending a meditation class, or deliberately inviting grace by creating a ceremony or ritual around an area in your life where you feel stuck and wish to heal.

## Personal Reflection on Faith

Have you ever experienced a moment of grace or a time where you felt "touched" by God? Reflect on the power of that moment. What message did it bring? Can you apply that message today?

_____

_____

_____

_____

_____

_____

_____

_____

_____

_____

_____

_____

_____

# Day 18

## Embrace the Darkness

*People are like stained-glass windows. They sparkle and shine when the sun is out, but when the darkness sets in, their true beauty is revealed only if there is a light from within.*

~ Elisabeth Kübler-Ross

*You do not need to know precisely what is happening, or exactly where it is all going. What you need is to recognize the possibilities and challenges offered by the present moment and to embrace them with courage, faith, and hope.*

~ Thomas Merton

I often use the metaphor of walking through the wilderness, where it is dark and the path is not clear, to describe your journey through grief. Yet it is precisely this act—walking into the darkness of your grief—that helps you reconcile your loss. When you embrace your pain, you in turn honor your pain. It is this honoring that will eventually, slowly, allow you to come alive again. When you heal, you will integrate your grief into yourself and learn to live a full and meaningful life once again.

It takes courage and faith to commit to embracing the darkness. It's hard when you are in pain to resist the urge to turn away and distract yourself. After all, our society has taught you to avoid pain—and it provides a myriad of ways to do so! With alternate realities literally at your fingertips in the form of media devices large and small, you could go through life hardly present to your pain. It takes a conscious commitment to make space for your dark, hard feelings to surface and an inner strength to "be with" them and to "sit in your wound."

I have found through my years of companioning mourners that they often want to rush grief and mourning. It's understandable. It's unpleasant to feel "weak" or "out of control," as society often defines it. It is tiring to cry and feel drained by sadness. People often ask me, "How long will my grief last?" They are anxious to get "back to normal." Yet the only way to feel right again emotionally, spiritually, and even physically is to slowly

*When you walk to the edge of all the light you have and take that first step into the darkness of the unknown, you must believe that one of two things will happen. There will be something solid for you to stand upon, or you will be taught to fly.*

~ Patrick Overton

*Faith is like radar that sees through the fog—the reality of things at a distance that the human eye cannot see.*

~ Corrie Ten Boom

navigate your way through the darkness, acknowledging all the sights, smells, sounds, and feelings it brings.

It's the only route to true healing. If you avoid your grief and stuff it, you will discover over time that the pain of your grief will keep trying to get your attention. In the long run, ignoring your grief is even more painful. It is a slow closing off of your heart to yourself and to others. It is accepting a half-fulfilled life and brings a sense that you yourself are dying while you are alive.

When you set an intention to heal, on the other hand, you take an active role in grieving and mourning. When feelings arise, you accept them and express them. You seek out people and organized activities that offer a safe environment to release your grief through mourning. You honor your journey through the dark wilderness.

Ask God or the Universe to help you take this journey. When you stumble or get lost, call on your faith to bushwhack a path for you. Of course, there will be times when you need to take a break and regain your strength. It's impossible to embrace all your pain at once. Instead, "dose" your pain. Invite it to come to you in small doses then allow it to retreat until you feel ready to take it on again.

## Personal Reflection on Faith

What habits do you have that can distract you from your grief feelings? Plan to cut down on these activities and instead take some time to sit in silence with your pain or write about your journey.

_____

_____

_____

_____

_____

_____

_____

_____

_____

_____

_____

_____

# Day 19

Invite Love

*Believe in a love that is being stored up for you like an inheritance, and have faith that in this love there is a strength and a blessing so large that you can travel as far as you wish without having to step outside it.*

~ Rainer Maria Rilke

*Love without hope will not survive.*
*Love without faith changes nothing.*
*Love gives power to hope and faith.*

~ Toba Beta

Love is the door through which faith enters. In many religions and spiritual movements, God is equivalent to love. Some people define God as the force of love and goodness in our world and in the universe—the genesis of all life.

In love we often find healing. Unconditional love—accepting and loving others fully regardless of who they are and what they might have done—is one of the greatest gifts you can give to another and another can give to you.

If the person who died was your source of unconditional love, you most likely feel as if your heart has been damaged. Yet the force of love does not live in just this one person. It may seem impossible, but you need to reach out to others who can also offer you love. You will never be able to replace your loved one and the powerful connection you shared, but you can discover a new expression of love in someone else. Children are excellent sources of unconditional love. So are dear friends who know you best and love you just the way you are. Parents, siblings, and children can also give you unconditional love. Sometimes even people you just met—perhaps whom you find in a healing environment like a place of worship or support group—can offer a loving ear or a shoulder to lean on. If you attend a grief support group, you will be doubly comforted by the fact that everyone there understands you and most likely feels just as you do. There is power in this group experience.

*Love only fails when we fail to love.*

~ Tyler Edwards

Let people in. Allow their love to wash over you, to seep into the cracks in your heart. Don't fall into the trap of thinking that needing love is a sign of weakness. Many people find it easier to give than to receive. Practice receiving. Call a supportive friend and tell him you need to talk. Trust that if you pour out your heart, your friend will accept what you have to say. A part of opening to love is daring to speak your truth. Approach your meeting with an open heart, and allow yourself to take in the words and expression of love that your friend offers.

It is also important that you practice self-love during this time. Pretend you are your best friend and comfort her. What would you say or do to show her your love? What would you encourage her to do? You might suggest she take a lot of naps and walks, indulge in massages, see a counselor, seek spiritual support from a pastor or friend, and so on. You might simply sit with her and hold her as she cries. Give yourself this comfort. The demands of grief can take their toll on you. Remember, love is food for the soul.

# Personal Reflection on Faith

With whom in your life are you open to sharing your heart?
Call that person today.

_____

_____

_____

_____

_____

_____

_____

_____

_____

_____

_____

_____

# Day 20

## Honor Your Sixth Sense

*Sometimes beautiful things come into our
lives out of nowhere. We can't always
understand them, but we have to trust in them.
I know you want to question everything, but
sometimes it pays to just have a little faith.*

~ Lauren Kate

*For me the sweetest contact with God has no form.
I close my eyes, look within, and enter a deep, soft
silence. The infinity of God's creation embraces me.*

~ Michael Jackson

The dictionary defines the "sixth sense" as "a power of perception beyond the five senses; intuition." I also like to think of it as the language of our soul, or divine spark. We use our sixth sense to connect with the realm of God and the greater, grand whole. With it, we tap into this spiritual world on both a conscious and unconscious level. I encourage you to access your sixth sense and to follow your intuition during this time of uncertainty. More than ever, it is when we are suffering that our souls wish to speak.

Do you believe in angels? The Catholic Church teaches that everyone has a guardian angel. Muslims believe God created "heavenly angels." The New Age movement professes that angels are a high vibration in our world and that they communicate directly with God. Many faiths believe all of us can call on angels for guidance at any time.

Have you ever had a stranger tell you something completely out of the blue, but it was exactly what you needed to hear at the time? Or, maybe you've had a good friend call right when you needed him most? Maybe they were acting as angels, or were inspired by angels, to care for you.

Personally, I sometimes sense a committee of angels in my head. I have heard them cheer when I have a spiritual or emotional breakthrough or a profound thought about myself

*All I have seen teaches me to trust the Creator for all I have not seen.*

~ Ralph Waldo Emerson

and the direction of my life. Sometimes they even seem to tease me by laughing at my foibles—but only in the most loving way.

You may also have strange or repetitive dreams during this time. Maybe you dream you are searching for the person who died, or talking with him. Accept these dreams as opportunities to experience being with him again and to integrate the reality of the death.

Go exploring. Peruse the spirituality or religion shelves of a bookstore or library and pick up books that spark your interest. Try a meditation or yoga class. Attend a spiritual seminar or explore a new place of worship. Create some art. Get out your camera and take landscape photographs, or bring your sketchpad or paints to a national park. Travel to a new town, state, or country. Go on a roadtrip to visit an old friend. Being in new places and doing new activities opens us to new ways of thinking. When we stretch ourselves we are more open, and we use our senses more acutely.

Open to the mystery. If you don't know where to start, try hanging out in "thin" places. In the Celtic tradition "thin places" are areas where the separation between the physical world and the spiritual world become tenuous—where water and land meet or land and sky come together. Experience the sunset or sunrise. Overlook a grand vista. Float on a lake and watch the sunlight shimmer on the water. Gaze at the horizon.

# Personal Reflection on Faith

Think about times when you "knew" something or had a spiritual epiphany or sensed the presence of someone who has died. Which elements were in place that turned on your sixth sense?

_____

_____

_____

_____

_____

_____

_____

_____

_____

_____

_____

_____

# Day 21

## Find Balance

*Life is grace. Sleep is forgiveness. The night absolves. Darkness wipes the slate clean, not spotless to be sure, but clean enough for another day's chalking.*

~ Frederick Buechner

*I cheated on my fears, broke up with my doubts, got engaged to my faith, and now I'm marrying my dreams.*

~ Anonymous

Life is a balancing act. When I was raising my children, we would often contemplate daily choices. We would go through scenarios, like "If you choose to play that game all afternoon, you won't have time to get your chores done before your soccer game." I find that people in general are happy when life is balanced and sometimes become stressed or anxious when it's not. Eating well without too many indulgences, sleeping well with just the occasional late night, doing the tasks at hand before spending too much time playing or relaxing—all these choices lead to balance. Balancing our lives demands us to live consciously.

Get in the habit of checking in with yourself on all levels—spiritually, emotionally, socially, mentally, and physically—on a regular basis. In the middle of the day, stop and ask, "How am I feeling? Is there something I need? Why am I feeling off-kilter? What will bring me back to center?" "Check ins" throughout the day will not only help keep you balanced but will help you live intentionally. When you live intentionally, you make choices to set the course for your day and, eventually, your life.

Sometimes people need help to get back in balance. Daily rituals can provide a structure that you can relax into—for example, saying the same prayer each morning, listening to inspiring podcasts on your daily drive to work, or taking a regular walk with your dog. So does having a set place to go

*Believe there is a great power silently working all things for good.*

~ Beatrix Potter


*Faith is not Desire. Faith is Will. Desires are things that need to be satisfied, whereas Will is a force. Will changes the space around us.*

~ Paulo Coelho

to feed your spirit, like a place of worship, a support group, a counselor, a weekly meeting with a friend, an exercise class, a study group, a hiking club, a volunteer job, and more.

Consider whether or not you've fallen into any bad habits or unfulfilling routines—things that fill time but are void of meaning or self-destructive—such as drinking too much or spending every evening on the couch in front of the television. It is easy, when you feel a need for comfort, to turn to the wrong things because they are immediate and don't demand anything from you. Stop and take a look. If you have fallen into an unhealthy habit, name one or two steps you can take right now—and each day forward—to lessen its hold on you.

Nourish your grieving soul by giving attention to those things that fill your life with richness. Tune in to your divine spark, and figure a plan to move toward fulfilling your soul's destiny. Consider making a regular date with yourself to go into "exile." Spend this time being by yourself in silence or in nature. Allow yourself to do and think nothing. It's in this silence that our souls often step forward. The training of prajna is at the heart of Buddhism. Prajna means wisdom, insight, and enlightenment. Prajna emerges when your mind is pure and calm.

Let the steady force of living on purpose in your daily life buoy you and keep you upright.

## Personal Reflection on Faith

In what areas do you feel off-balance? Close your eyes for a few minutes and contemplate possible solutions by asking yourself what you need to feel centered again.

_____

_____

_____

_____

_____

_____

_____

_____

_____

_____

_____

# Day 22

## Seek Enlightenment

*As we let our light shine, we unconsciously give other people permission to do the same. As we are liberated from our own fear, our presence actually liberates others.*

~ Marianne Williamson

*Always keep your mind as bright and clear as the vast sky, the great ocean, and the highest peak, empty of all thoughts. Always keep your body filled with light and heat. Fill yourself with the power of wisdom and enlightenment.*

~ Morihei Ueshiba

Many religions explore the idea of enlightenment. To be enlightened is to have "spiritual or intellectual insight." In Buddhism, to be enlightened is to have reached "Nirvana"—a supreme state free of suffering and individual existence. While Christianity does not generally call on the concept of enlightenment, the Bible does refer to "revelation"—a manifestation of divine will or truth.

Let's break enlightenment down even further. Many spiritual movements and religions use light as a symbol of the spiritual world. For example, the Quakers refer to the light of God as being in every person and encourage followers to be guided by the light to achieve a full relationship with God. The idea that light represents a good, healing force and darkness the opposite is woven throughout every culture in the world, and it shows up consistently in our religions, writings, and artwork. At its base, I can't help think of the sun and how its light is the source of all life on earth.

So, how can you bring light—spiritual enlightenment—into your life? For starters, simply go outside and feel the sun shining on your face. Imagine its light and warmth seeping into all of your pores and healing you—mind, body, and soul. Next, seek out activities that feed hopeful emotions, like joy, peace, calm, balance, love, and serenity. Common ways people seek these "light" emotions are meditating, practicing yoga, being in nature, laughing with a friend, playing sports or games, singing, dancing, praying, and making music.

*Come forth into the light of things,*
*let nature be your teacher.*

~ William Wordsworth

*Believe more deeply. Hold your face up to the light,*
*even though for the moment you do not see.*

~ Bill Wilson

If you feel a bit like you are bursting with your grief and need and want spiritual answers, you might consider going on a spiritual quest of sorts. The purpose of a spiritual quest is to take inventory of your spiritual beliefs and decide what fits for you and what doesn't. More so, this journey is to come into your own as a spiritual being—a spiritual awakening complete with "aha" moments that significantly shape your spiritual beliefs and outlook, and most of all, connect you to God.

Many Native American cultures make "vision quests" a part of a child's coming-of-age. Vision quests often involve spending time alone in nature to commune with nature's forces and the spiritual energy of all of creation. During this time, the young person has a vision that reveals the purpose and destiny of his life.

Modern spiritual quests can take many forms. Some people read everything they can about different religions or explore new ways of thinking, such as those presented by the New Age movement, Native American teachings, and more. You might consider attending a spiritual retreat, experiencing a sweat lodge, spending time at a monastery, traveling to a spiritual place such as Mecca or Jerusalem, spending extended time alone in nature, and more.

Going through the grief and mourning process after someone you deeply love has died is, in itself, a version of a spiritual quest. Grief is a profound experience that can strip you bare and cause you to seek spiritual wholeness on a new level.

## Personal Reflection on Faith

How can you "shine light" on your grief or connect to the "light of God" today?

_____

_____

_____

_____

_____

_____

_____

_____

_____

_____

_____

_____

# Day 23

## Carry a Touchstone

*Even the merest gesture is holy if it is filled with faith.*
~ Franz Kafka


*You can't confuse childlike faith with childish thinking.*
~ John F. MacArthur, Jr.

Bring faith into your everyday life by attaching it to an object or symbol—a touchstone—that represents a spiritual intention. Maybe right now you need to be reminded to open to grief. Select a symbol that represents openness for you. Or maybe you need to be reminded of the steadfastness and strength that your faith brings. Display an object of your faith somewhere you can see it often during the day—on your kitchen table, work desk, or dashboard. When you see it, think: "Have faith," "Believe," or another word or short phrase that helps bring you back on track.

Another helpful habit is carrying a stone or charm as a touchstone. Whenever you feel a need to re-center or reconnect with your touchstone's meaning, you can reach in your pocket and touch it. Rubbing the smooth surface will calm you and remind you of your spiritual intention. Novelty stores often sell such items. I was in a small shop recently that had a basket of charms on the counter—small, round, smooth metal disks that had a Chinese symbol on one side and its matching English word on the other. Words like faith, integrity, believe, balance, strength, tranquility, trust, and honesty were represented. You can also visit a nature store and sift through the bins of polished rocks or gems to find one that draws you.

Other items can also be used as symbols or instruments to center you and remind you of your spiritual wishes. For example, sound, and the vibrations it creates, can be a powerful healing

*The problem with certainty is that it is static; it can do little but endlessly reassert itself. Uncertainty, by contrast, is full of unknowns [and] possibilities....*

~ Stephen Batchelor

*Faith is not so much something we believe; faith is something we live.*

~ Joseph B. Wirthlin

and centering tool. The vibrations of sound awaken your neurological system—in other words, sound gets your energies flowing. This is precisely why many cultures use drums as a part of their spiritual ceremonies. Native Americans believe that drums speak. They see the drum as akin to a beating heart—that of the drummer and Mother Earth. African tribes use drums to summon spirits to assist in positive change and healing. Consider getting a bongo drum or even a simple set of drumsticks. Chimes, bells, gongs, symbols, singing bowls, and tuning forks also resonate with many spiritual practices.

Besides instruments of sound, explore symbols from your religious faith or spiritual practice, such as rosary beads, crosses, prayer beads, Buddhas, crystals, angels, gemstones, and more. The key is selecting a symbol that excites your spirit. Remember to spend some quiet time contemplating the spiritual meaning of your touchstone and assigning a word, phrase, or short prayer to represent its meaning.

# Personal Reflection on Faith

Name a spiritual intention or characteristic you would like to set forth or bring into your life. Does a touchstone come to mind to represent that intention?

_____

_____

_____

_____

_____

_____

_____

_____

_____

_____

_____

_____

_____

# Day 24

## Practice Acceptance

*Acceptance of one's life has nothing to do with resignation; it does not mean running away from the struggle. On the contrary, it means accepting it as it comes, with all the handicaps of heredity, of suffering, of psychological complexes, and injustices.*

~ Paul Tournier

*I don't think that we're meant to understand it all the time. I think that sometimes we just have to have faith.*

~ Nicholas Sparks

When someone dies, the first response of those close to the person is a resounding, "No!" Death is an abrupt ending, even when anticipated. There is an immediate loss of connection and a feeling of disbelief—how can the person you shared your days with be gone? How could he be here one minute and gone the next? The last thing you want to do is accept the death. Yet acceptance is a necessary part of healing, or reconciling, your loss. It usually doesn't happen immediately, of course. It's best to let it unfold naturally, regardless of how much time it takes. You may first feel numbness, disbelief, and even denial about the death. This is normal. But soon you will come to acknowledge the death with your mind, and later with your heart.

Acceptance is a step toward reconciling your loss. Reconciliation comes after you have journeyed through grief and examined and experienced your feelings of pain and loss, and have expressed them through active mourning. (By active mourning I mean that you have spent time talking, writing, crying, running, painting, dancing, serving, and thinking out your grief.) Reconciling the death doesn't mean you resolve it; you never get over the death of someone close to you. Think of reconciliation as integrating your loss. The experience of knowing the person who died, having her die, and feeling the effects of her death will always live inside you and be a part of you. Accepting that she died, and accepting you must go on without her, comes before

*Every tomorrow has two handles. We can take hold of it with the handle of anxiety or the handle of faith.*

~ Henry Ward Beecher

*The first step toward change is awareness. The second step is acceptance.*

~ Nathaniel Branden

reconciliation. When you reconcile your grief, the joy of life will pop out behind the clouds, and you will feel a renewed sense of meaning and purpose in life.

Acceptance also forces the hand of forgiveness. Sometimes death brings mixed feelings. While you probably felt love for the person who died, most relationships are not made up of 100 percent happy, healthy times. Were there small or significant events, conflicts, disagreements, or hurts that went unresolved between you and the person who died? If so, your grieving process might feel harder. While it is not necessary to forgive the person for past wrongs, if your faith teaches that forgiveness is freeing and will bring you closer to God, it might be something you want to explore.

If you cannot find forgiveness in your heart, it's OK. You need to live your truth, regardless. If you do come to forgiveness, please don't feel like it is too late to tell the person. Say it out loud for him to hear, or write a letter and send it to his old address—even if it will simply bounce around the mail system forever. The same goes for the opposite. If you want forgiveness, go ahead and ask for it.

Forgiveness and acceptance have the power to resolve feelings of guilt, shame, anger, resentment, blame, and fear. If you harbor these challenging feelings, know that they can be a natural part of grief, but you may need a professional counselor to help you work through them.

## Personal Reflection on Faith

Acceptance is a theme throughout your grief journey. First you accept the death, then you accept your path toward healing, finally you accept your new future. Where are you in this process of acceptance?

_____

_____

_____

_____

_____

_____

_____

_____

_____

_____

_____

_____

# Day 25

## Welcome Flashes of Joy

*Joy is the infallible sign of the presence of God.*
~ Pierre Teilhard de Chardin


*Profound joy of the heart is like a magnet
that indicates the path of life.*
~ Mother Teresa

When you lose someone you love, it can be hard to tap into joy. You may be thinking, "Joy? Happiness? Those are the last emotions I feel!" Yet joy has a way of catching you by surprise. When you least expect it, a flash of joy can burst into your daily life. Maybe it's a grandchild's smile, a bluebird on a branch, or a memory of your loved one's face in a moment of sheer excitement or joy.

Joy can also come at your darkest moments. Sometimes as we mourn and share our pain, a friend does something or says something that makes us laugh. A woman I know who endured breast cancer told of how after she was diagnosed, she and a good friend went shopping to get her mind off things. As they sorted through racks of clothes, her friend would hold up everything pink she could find—crazy shirts, ugly dresses, goofy scarves. Soon enough they were laughing in the aisles.

Experiencing flashes of joy and laughter can bring relief, calm, and normalcy to life when it feels at its most surreal. It can restore faith that things will be OK. Moments of joy give you strength to carry on.

Avoid the trap of thinking that laughing and having fun is somehow a betrayal of the person who died. Laughing does not deny your mourning or mean that you don't miss the person who died. Feel peace in knowing that if your loved one is looking down upon you, he is smiling at your moments of

*Faith is what makes life bearable, with all its tragedies*
*and ambiguities and sudden, startling joys.*

~ Madeleine L'Engle

*Joy and sorrow are inseparable…together they*
*come and when one sits alone with you…*
*remember that the other is asleep upon your bed.*

~ Kahlil Gibran

joy, saying "Yes! That's the ticket!" Recall the love you shared and know that this person would want you to heal and feel joy again.

Think of these moments of joy as flashes of light in the darkness of your suffering. They reveal your pain, yet they also give you hope that light (and love and laughter) do exist. Someday your moments of joy will come more frequently and closer together. Believe this. You will not always feel this much pain and loss. You will probably always grieve for your loved one, but it won't be this raw. For now, let these spontaneous moments of joy carry this promise from one day to the next. Eventually you will be able to string them together to create a more constant happiness.

*It is good to laugh. Laughter is spiritual relaxation.*
~ Abdu'l-Baha

## Personal Reflection on Faith

When was the last time you felt spontaneous joy? Remember, and let yourself smile. Or recall a joyous memory of the person who died. Let this light feeling feed your faith so that you can endure.

_____

_____

_____

_____

_____

_____

_____

_____

_____

_____

_____

_____

# Day 26

## Summon Hope

*I plead with you—never, ever give up on hope, never doubt, never tire, and never become discouraged. Be not afraid.*

~ Pope John Paul II

*Never lose faith in yourself, and never lose hope; remember, even when this world throws its worst and then turns its back, there is still always hope.*

~ Pittacus Lore

Hope and faith are intrinsically tied and even sometimes used interchangeably. Hope is the feeling that things will turn out for the best. It is trust in a goodness that is yet to be. Faith is also confidence or trust in something. I've heard someone say the difference is that hope always looks to the future while faith happens in the here and now. You might hope or wish for something to be true, but if you have faith, you know it is true already. Hope is a promise; faith is a conviction.

The beauty of hope is that it keeps you going. Hope motivates you to move toward a future state that you want to achieve and allows for the birth of faith. The more you hope for something, the more you build steam toward it. The closer you get, the stronger your faith becomes that you are achieving what you want.

What is it that you hope for right now? Think about that for a moment. Are you hoping that you will not always feel such debilitating pain over the loss of the person who died? Know that you won't. Rest assured that while time does not automatically heal your grief, if you are embracing your grief feelings rather than turning away from them, the pain will eventually subside and be replaced with peace and even joy.

You may miss the person terribly and wish you could see her again. Do the next best thing. Look through photo albums or watch old videos of her. Or do something to honor her spirit,

*To have faith is to be sure of the things we hope for, to be certain of the things we cannot see.*

~ Hebrews 11:1

like engaging in an activity that she loved or working toward a cause that she believed in. These actions will give you hope for a better future.

Find hope in your everyday life. If it is hard to feel hope on your own, feed on other people's hopes for you and their faith in your healing. Or draw strength from the persistency of the natural world: spring comes, the sun rises, clouds break, the earth warms, and flowers burst from seeds. You are a part of this natural cycle of life, death, and rebirth. Have faith in this. You, too, are moving toward a new beginning.

*I find hope in the darkest of days and focus in the brightest. I do not judge the universe.*

~ Dalai Lama

# Personal Reflection on Faith

Consider what you hope for and what you have faith in regarding your grief journey.

_____

_____

_____

_____

_____

_____

_____

_____

_____

_____

_____

_____

_____

# Day 27

## Expect Silver Linings

*No pain that we suffer, no trial that we experience, is wasted. It ministers to our education, to the development of such qualities as patience, faith, fortitude, and humility. All that we suffer and all that we endure, especially when we endure it patiently, builds up our characters, purifies our hearts, expands our souls, and makes us more tender and charitable, more worthy to be called the children of God.*

~ Orson F. Whitney

*I am fundamentally an optimist. Whether that comes from nature or nurture, I cannot say. Part of being optimistic is keeping one's head pointed toward the sun, one's feet moving forward. There were many dark moments when my faith in humanity was sorely tested, but I would not and could not give myself up to despair.*

~ Nelson Mandela

Of course you would never choose to have someone you care about die, and no one would wish that suffering upon you. Yet it can't be denied: pain and sorrow do provide opportunities for growth and offer gifts of wisdom and strength. No doubt, you would trade in these new gifts to have your loved one back again, but since that is not possible, focus on the silver lining of your loss.

Maybe your faith has deepened through your grief experience. Or maybe living alone has made you more independent and confident in your own abilities. Do you reach out more to others now than you used to? If so, has it strengthened your sense of community, your bonds of friendship, or your faith in humanity? Have you discovered some new habits or activities that bring you meaning and joy?

If you believe in an afterlife, you probably have faith that you will get to continue your spiritual relationship with the person who died. As Robert Benchley wrote, "Death ends a life, not a relationship." Start now by talking to the person who died, reviewing memories, and keeping his spirit alive by living life as he would have done. Let this be a silver lining.

When I lost my father to cancer, it was a time of great pain as well as great spiritual growth. Often I had to draw on my "Higher Self" for strength. I see my Higher Self as my wise, divine spark—my spirit—that is stripped of my ego and

*Well, it's true that I have been hurt in my life. Quite a bit. But it's also true that I have loved, and been loved, and that carries a weight of its own. A greater weight, in my opinion. It's like a pie chart. In the end, I'll look back on my life and see that the greatest piece of it was love. The problems, the divorces, the sadness...those will be there too, but just smaller slivers, tiny pieces.*

~ Sarah Dessen

answers to a higher calling of truth, strength, and wisdom. When I am in my Higher Self, I know that all situations in life are learning opportunities, and that out of darkness comes light. I encourage you to tap into your "Higher Self" as best you can during this time. While it's difficult to see the silver lining of your loss at face value, have faith that your soul experiences it on a higher plane—with a watchful eye toward evolving and growing.

Silver linings are best seen in hindsight. If you are deep in the muck of your grief, you will find it impossible to imagine that anything good could come out of this. That's OK. Stay in the muck. But know that someday you will emerge, and you'll be able to see that even though you were mired in darkness, somehow a piece of your soul was washed clean.

*As the essence of courage is to stake one's life on a possibility, so the essence of faith is to believe the possibility exists.*

~ William Salter

## Personal Reflection on Faith

Have you identified any silver linings through your loss? If you are still too close to the death, think about silver linings that shined through during other challenging times in your life.

_____

_____

_____

_____

_____

_____

_____

_____

_____

_____

_____

_____

# Day 28

## Act on Your Faith

*But there were some things I believed in. Some things I had faith in. And faith isn't about perfect attendance to services or how much money you put on the little plate. It isn't about going skyclad to the Holy Rites or meditating each day upon the divine. Faith is about what you do. It's about aspiring to be better and nobler and kinder than you are. It's about making sacrifices for the good of others—even when there's not going to be anyone telling you what a hero you are.*

~ Jim Butcher

*True faith manifests itself through our actions.*

~ Francis Chan

If you are finding it hard to get out of bed some days, let alone go to the soup kitchen and volunteer, try going into autopilot. While it's appropriate and necessary for you to withdraw from the world for a time, it's also essential that you reengage sooner than later. The final need in the Six Needs of Mourning is to let others support you in your journey. And the only way this can happen is for you to make contact.

So if you have a breakfast date with a friend but dread getting dressed and out the door, stop seeing it as a choice and instead see it as a must-do and move forward. Be a robot: Wash your face, brush your teeth, get dressed, grab your keys, and head out the door with nary a thought of whether or not you want to go. The truth of the matter is you will most likely feel better afterward. You will most likely feel more hopeful than you did before. It's the old "put one foot in front of the other" cliché. And it works.

The same goes for practicing your faith. After a reasonable period of time away, at least try going through the motions of your faith—attend services, participate in prayer group, or sing in the choir. By continuing to participate in life, you will gain courage to face your grief and momentum to continue living. Get into the routine of doing activities that feed your spirit and your personal faith—like meditation, yoga, prayer, time in nature, time with people who inspire you and comfort you, and so on. If you feel better and more whole than before you started, it's worth doing. (The opposite is also true: If it feels bad and perhaps no longer "right," it's either too soon or it's not worth doing anymore.)

*This is my living faith, an active faith, a faith of verbs: to question, explore, experiment, experience, walk, run, dance, play, eat, love, learn, dare, taste, touch, smell, listen, speak, write, read, draw, provoke, emote, scream, sin, repent, cry, kneel, pray, bow, rise, stand, look, laugh, cajole, create, confront, confound, walk back, walk forward, circle, hide, and seek.*

~ Terry Tempest Williams

*Faith is about doing. You are how you act, not just how you believe.*

~ Mitch Albom

Many people I have counseled have found it healing to "act out" their loved one's convictions and to continue on their projects. One man I know created a scholarship at his mother's alma mater for students pursuing teaching, as she did. One woman took over her husband's restaurant and carried on his community projects that were tied to the business. Another woman traveled to Africa to fulfill a dream of her husband's to study elephants there; she brought some of his ashes along to spread on the elephants' savannah.

Maybe your religious faith or personal convictions tell you that it's important to help others. The Golden Rule in Christianity to "do unto others as you would have them do unto you" is a common theme in all major religions. The Bahá'í, Quaker, and Unitarian faiths put great emphasis on social justice, peace, and making the world a better place. Getting out and acting on these principles is good for your soul. Studies show that people who volunteer are happier than those who don't and that volunteers often gain as many benefits as they provide. As humans, it's in our DNA to rely on, and care for, other humans. If you've volunteered in the past, get back to it. If you are new to volunteering, contemplate which social cause you feel strongest about and research ways to get involved.

It doesn't have to be that formal. It can be as simple as committing to help an elderly neighbor or babysitting a friend's kids or your grandkids. Helping others strengthens your faith in the joy and meaningfulness of life, even without the person who died.

## Personal Reflection on Faith

Which single action could you take today to honor your faith or strengthen your spirit?

_____

_____

_____

_____

_____

_____

_____

_____

_____

_____

_____

# Day 29

## Trust in a Brighter Future

*If we were logical, the future would be bleak, indeed. But we are more than logical. We are human beings, and we have faith, and we have hope, and we can work.*

~ Jacques Cousteau

*Faith is not the clinging to a shrine but an endless pilgrimage of the heart.*

~ Abraham Joshua Heschel

The phrase "this too shall pass" offers encouragement for the future. It has its roots deep in history. The original use is thought to be by Persian Sufi poets in the 1100s, and some believe it was included in a Jewish folktale about King Solomon. Today it travels around religious and spiritual circles as a message of hope: this pain, this situation, like everything else in life, will pass. While you will always grieve the death of the person who died, the intensity of it will shift and change as you grow through time. Have faith that this too shall pass and a brighter future will come—as long as you want it and do the necessary, hard work of grieving and mourning.

Commit to opening your heart to your grief and your hope for the future. Your suffering will transform you, as long as you embrace it. Remember how much you have gained from loving the person who died. The alternative to living fully and loving deeply is living a life of apathy. Apathy literally means that you are unable to suffer. In order to not suffer, you disengage from others and fill your time with distraction. Make a conscious choice to stay truly alive! If it helps, think about how the person who died lives on through you and your actions and deeds. Vow to stay conscious of your desire to live deeply for both of you.

It is moments that turn into hours that turn into days that become our futures. As you stay honest, raw, and real in the

*To find the point where hypothesis and fact meet; the delicate equilibrium between dream and reality; the place where fantasy and earthly things are metamorphosed into a work of art; the hour when faith in the future becomes knowledge of the past....to accept uncertainties quietly, even our incomplete knowledge of God; this is what man's journey is about, I think.*

~ Lillian Smith

moment, you create a future filled with meaning, purpose, and real connections replete with joy and love.

Take a minute to think about what brings your life meaning. Is it deeply connecting with those you care about? Making a difference in the world? Feeling at ease in your own skin? Now, devise a plan of how to bring more of these activities and values into your life. Keep it simple. Break it down into small steps. For example, you could commit to calling or seeing your child, sibling, parent, or a special friend once a week. Make a bulleted list of five items that bring you meaning and put it on your fridge or bathroom mirror. Consider it your "vision statement" and see it as a working plan to get to a better, brighter place.

*The future can be anything we want it to be, providing we have the faith...*
~ Charles F. Kettering

## Personal Reflection on Faith

What's the first item you would put on a list of what makes your life matter? How can you bring more of that into your days?

_____

_____

_____

_____

_____

_____

_____

_____

_____

_____

_____

_____

# Day 30

Leap

*I have come to accept the feeling of not knowing where I am going. And I have trained myself to love it. Because it is only when we are suspended in mid-air, with no landing in sight, that we force our wings to unravel and begin our flight. And as we fly, we still may not know where we are going to. But the miracle is in the unfolding of the wings. You may not know where you're going, but you know that so long as you spread your wings, the winds will carry you.*

~ C. JoyBell C.

*Leap, and the net will appear.*

~ Julia Cameron

I have always loved the idea of taking a leap of faith. Just the idea of leaping—legs sprawled, arms flung high—and the assuredness of that act despite the possibility of falling seems so freeing and full of promise. Leaping also holds the possibility of big change and growth—one minute you are there, and the next you are here, in a new place with new confidence and new opportunities.

The metaphor "leap of faith" was first used by the 19th century Danish philosopher Soren Kierkegaard. He saw the space between God and man as a gulf that could only be bridged by faith; to fully connect with God, people were required to leap the gulf—to take that big step from the known into the unknown, a step that requires faith.

You can never know for certain what God's plan is for you and the people you love. Yet you can trust the truth in your heart and believe what you think are the right answers. When you feel certain of the answers, you've leaped. You've established faith. Let the certainty of your faith carry you.

I have faith that love and joy are synonymous with God—and are part of our true purposes on earth—to give and to receive love and joy. You may believe that your purpose is to leave a mark on this world by positively influencing a social change or simply supporting others so they can thrive. Whatever you believe, own it as yours and let it define you. Let it help you

*You are never dedicated to something you have complete confidence in. No one is fanatically shouting that the sun is going to rise tomorrow. They know it's going to rise tomorrow.*

~ Robert M. Pirsig

live out your days with meaning and move forward through your grief.

Dealing with the death of someone close to you is in itself a series of "leaps." Figuring out a new daily routine without her is a leap. Stepping out of your comfort zone of the roles you have always played as husband, father, mother, wife, or child is a leap. You leap when you decide to try something new—something you know will help you heal and grow. You leap when you decide to descend downward into the depths of your pain and release it through your tears. For grief is not a steady, upward journey but a meandering, challenging hike of hills and valleys. Being willing to have faith that you will find reconciliation and be able to feel real joy again is possibly the greatest leap of all.

I encourage you to leap when an opportunity that holds promise presents itself. Feel your faith in a good outcome like a ball of light inside your chest. Be comforted by its warmth and its wisdom that if you leap, it will grow brighter. Choose life! Leap!

## Personal Reflection on Faith

What are some small leaps you've taken lately? Do you feel larger, more significant leaps brewing inside of you? Call on your faith and make the jump. Feel the strength each leap brings.

_____

_____

_____

_____

_____

_____

_____

_____

_____

_____

_____

_____

*Closing Thoughts*

*Faith is the daring of the soul to go farther than it can see.*

~ William Newton Clarke

*Embrace an Attitude of Faith as You Continue Your Journey*

I appreciate the chance to play a small part in your journey through grief and mourning. I commend you for seeking ways to embrace your grief rather than taking the advice of our grief-adverse society and turning away from it and "getting over it" quickly and efficiently. Your dedication to healing is evident in the simple fact that you've read this book.

Some people define "doing well" as not showing any outward signs of grief. If you are stoic, others might call you "strong" and compliment you on how well you have handled your grief. Please know that the opposite is true. The real strength lies in you calling upon your hope, mustering your courage, and taking continual leaps of faith as you mourn—that is, express outside yourself—the deep sadness and pain of losing someone you love. You will find that although grief doesn't have a neat, precise ending, it will get easier as time passes and as you continue to acknowledge the death, embrace the pain, remember the person who died, explore your new self-identity, search for meaning, and receive the support of others. Ironically, when grief is denied, it only gets more complicated and leads to what I call "living in the shadow of the ghosts of grief," which often means a life of ongoing depression, anxiety, disconnection, and, at a minimum, flatness.

I encourage you to let your divine spark embrace the divine spark of the person who died and rejoice in the beauty that you two shared. Honor her through your words and actions. Feeling your grief and expressing it is one way to do so; carrying out her passions is another. If you "experience" your loved one in some way that seems mystical or impossible—like the weight of his hand on your shoulder or his voice clear-as-a-bell in the next room—don't be scared or deny it. Accept it as a gift. On the same note, if you feel a need to do something unconventional, like having a ceremony in nature with friends, going on a trek on your own, or building a shrine in your house or garden, do it. Trust your intuition and emotions. They are the voice of your soul. Have faith that they will serve you well.

Believe that a new future—one you can't even imagine right now but are willing to bet on—exists for you. Right now you may only long for the past, but I want you to trust that brighter days are ahead. Honor your needs and your feelings along the way: cry, wail, yell, jump up-and-down, pray, dance, worship, write letters to the person who died, have ceremonies, whatever it takes to let your soul speak and feel your divine spark reignite, even for a moment. If you do this I have complete faith that one day you will reconcile your grief and once again, feel whole and alive: wholly alive. May this be true for you.

## Start a Faith-Filled Support Group!

This book makes an ideal 12-week support group text. Have a get-started session, then meet once a week for 10 weeks and discuss three of the reflections each meeting. Hold a final meeting based on the Closing Thoughts section.

## The Mourner's Book of Hope
### 30 Days of Inspiration

To integrate loss and to move forward with a life of meaning and love, you must have hope. Hope is a belief in a good that is yet to be. This beautiful little hardcover gift book offers Dr. Wolfelt's thoughts on hope in grief interspersed with quotes from the world's greatest hope-filled thinkers.

*Hope begins in the dark, the stubborn hope that if you just show up and try to do the right thing, the dawn will come. You wait and watch and work: you don't give up.* - Anne Lamott

*Sitting in the quietness of hope encourages me to discover so many reasons to live fully until I die.* - Alan D. Wolfelt

*When we become aware that we do not have to escape our pains, but that we can mobilize them into a common search for life, those very pains are transformed from expressions of despair into signs of hope.* - Henri Nouwen

ISBN 978-1-879651-65-4 • 200 pages • hardcover • $15.95

Companion
P R E S S

All Dr. Wolfelt's publications can be ordered by mail from:
Companion Press
3735 Broken Bow Road • Fort Collins, CO 80526
(970) 226-6050 • Fax 1-800-922-6051
www.centerforloss.com

# The Mourner's Book of Courage

## 30 Days of Encouragement

When someone you love dies, you must find within yourself the courage to embrace the pain and go on living without him or her. The word courage comes from the Old French word *corage*, which meant "heart" and "innermost feelings." In grief, you must open your heart to your innermost feelings and, instead of retreating from them, boldly befriend them. For it is in befriending your grief that you heal.

This book is written for those times in grief when you feel you don't have the courage to do the hard and necessary work of mourning. Written by Dr. Alan Wolfelt, it contains his compassionate words about finding courage deep within yourself. It also features quotes on *courage* from some of the world's greatest thinkers. *The Mourner's Book of Courage* will give you the dose of encouragement you need each day to not only survive your grief but go on to thrive and live life more deeply than you ever imagined.

ISBN 978-1-61722-154-5 • 200 pages • hardcover • $15.95

Companion
**PRESS**

All Dr. Wolfelt's publications can be ordered by mail from:
Companion Press
3735 Broken Bow Road • Fort Collins, CO 80526
(970) 226-6050 • Fax 1-800-922-6051
www.centerforloss.com

# Understanding Your Grief

### Ten Essential Touchstones for Finding Hope and Healing Your Heart

One of North America's leading grief educators, Dr. Alan Wolfelt has written many books about healing in grief. This book is his most comprehensive, covering the essential lessons that mourners have taught him in his three decades of working with the bereaved.

In compassionate, down-to-earth language, *Understanding Your Grief* describes ten touchstones—or trail markers—that are essential physical, emotional, cognitive, social, and spiritual signs for mourners to look for on their journey through grief.

The Ten Essential Touchstones:

1. Open to the presence of your loss.
2. Dispel misconceptions about grief.
3. Embrace the uniqueness of your grief.
4. Explore what you might experience.
5. Recognize you are not crazy.
6. Understand the six needs of mourning.
7. Nurture yourself.
8. Reach out for help.
9. Seek reconciliation, not resolution.
10. Appreciate your transformation.

ISBN 978-1-879651-35-7 • 176 pages • softcover • $14.95

Companion
PRESS

All Dr. Wolfelt's publications can be ordered by mail from:
Companion Press
3735 Broken Bow Road • Fort Collins, CO 80526
(970) 226-6050 • Fax 1-800-922-6051
www.centerforloss.com

To contact Dr. Wolfelt about speaking engagements or training opportunities at his Center for Loss and Life Transition, email him at DrWolfelt@centerforloss.com.